YOUR KNOWLEDGE HAS VALUE

Bibliographic information published by the German National Library:

The German National Library lists this publication in the National Bibliography; detailed bibliographic data are available on the Internet at http://dnb.dnb.de .

Imprint:

Copyright © 2017 GRIN Verlag, Open Publishing GmbH
Print and binding: Books on Demand GmbH, Norderstedt Germany
ISBN: 9783668533851

This book at GRIN:

http://www.grin.com/en/e-book/376002/hall-s-model-of-cultural-communication-economy-and-business-in-turkey

Hall's Model of Cultural Communication, Economy and Business in Turkey and the 7-D Model for analyzing Cultural Differences

GRIN Publishing

GRIN - Your knowledge has value

Since its foundation in 1998, GRIN has specialized in publishing academic texts by students, college teachers and other academics as e-book and printed book. The website www.grin.com is an ideal platform for presenting term papers, final papers, scientific essays, dissertations and specialist books.

"There is only one rule to remember when it comes to cultural differences – people may look at the same thing but they all see it differently, regardless of whether they come from the same or a different culture. This rule goes some way to explaining the diversity of the world"
(Yong & Baocheng, 2005)

Table of Contents

List of Abbreviations

CAGR	Compound Annual Growth Rate
Cf.	Confer (compare)
CIA	Central Intelligence Agency
DP	Democratic Party (Turkey)
e.g.	exempli gratia / for example
EU	European Union
f.	(and the) following (page)
ff.	(and the) following (pages)
GDP	Gross Domestic Product
HC	high-context
i.e.	id est / that is to say
IMF	International Monetary Fund
LC	low-context
MBO	Management by Objectives
OECD	Organization for Economic Co-operation and Development
PPP	Purchasing Power Parity
p.	Page
pp.	Pages
USD	United States Dollar (currency)
USA	United States of America
WWI	1st World War
WWII	2nd World War

List of Tables

List of Figures

1. Hall's Model of Cultural Communication – Outlining Business Cultures (France / USA)

1.1 Hall's Model of Cultural Communication

Edward T. Hall (1914-2009) was one of the first researchers in the field of intercultural communication. He stated that *"culture is communication."*[1] In his early works, he defined various concepts of space and demonstrated how people's use of it can affect cross-cultural behavior. This spatial approach in cultural differences resulted in the concept of *proxemics*. In *Hidden Dimension, Hall* also described *polychronic* and *monochronic* approaches to time. Lately, in *Beyond Culture* he identified the *context* dimension, which distinguishes between low-context (LC) and high-context (HC) cultures. To enable a basic understanding of *Halls* concept, the next parts will detailly explain the dimensions' *space, time* and *context*. Afterwards these will be used to compare *US* and *French* business cultures. It is necessary to say that in *Hall's* latest publications, he also described cultural differences in the *Speed of Messages, Information Flow* and the use of *Action Chains,* which won't be part of this essay.[2] The following explanations should help managers to use Hall's explanations in practice. However, one should be careful not to prejudice about individuals. Instead, these explanations can be used to gain sensibility for one's own culture and possible sources of conflict with others. Furthermore, they dispel the notion that there is one best way of doing things.[3]

1.1.1 Context

Context describes the information surrounding an event. Depending on the culture, the elements event and context combine in different proportions to produce a given meaning. In a *high-context* communication, most of the information is already within the person or environment - very little is in the coded, explicit, transmitted part of the message. In a *low-context* communication, most of the information is transferred by the explicit code. *Low-context* cultures

---

[1] Hall and Reed Hall (1990, p. 3)
[2] Cf. Hall and Reed Hall (1990, pp. 3–29); Rothlauf (2014, p. 32); Dumetz (2012); Berger and Hagemann (2011, p. 17); Müller and Gelbrich (2013, pp. 6–26); Hall (1973, 1969, 1963); Engelen and Tholen (2014, pp. 25–30); Gutting (2016, pp. 47–52); Kumbruck and Derboven (2016, pp. 28–29)
[3] Cf. Trompenaars and Hampden-Turner (2012, p. 3)

compartmentalize their personal relationships, work, and day-to-day life. Thus, they need background information each time they interact with others. HC cultures focus on interpersonal relations and extensive information networks. For most normal transactions in life they don't require, nor expect, much background information. *„High-context people are apt to become impatient and irritated when low-context people insist on giving them information they don't need. Conversely, low-context people are at a loss when high-context people do not provide enough information. One of the great communication challenges in life is to find the appropriate level of contexting needed in each situation. Too much information leads people to feel they are being talked down to; too little information can mystify them or make them feel left out. Ordinarily, people make these adjustments automatically in their own country, but in other countries their messages frequently miss the target."*[4] Any shift in the level of context is a communication: It can be indicating a warming of the relationship (upscale of context) or communicate displeasure (downscaling of context). In LC cultures, people can separate conflict issues from the person involved, they even perceive conflicts as instrumental in nature. In HC cultures, a conflict is almost always attached to people. As *Table 1* shows, the differences between high- and low-context cultures affect several parts of business. These assumptions are important for theorizing and researching about interpersonal conflict in an organizational setting. When people communicate cross-culturally, they need to know different communication patterns across cultures to resolve conflict situations.[5]

Factor	Low-Context Culture	High-Context Culture
Communication and language	Many overt and explicit messages are simple and clear	Many covert and implicit messages, with use of metaphor and reading between the lines
Dress Code	Dressing is highly individual and signals personality	Dressing follows a code, indicates position and signals status

---

[4] Hall and Reed Hall (1990, p. 9)
[5] Cf. Rothlauf (2014, pp. 32–33); Carté and Fox (2004, p. 18), Hall (1973); Hall and Reed Hall (1990, pp. 6–10); Müller and Gelbrich (2013, pp. 21–24); Hall and Reed Hall (1990, pp. 6–10); Blom and Meier (2004, pp. 93–95); Matveev (2016, pp. 93–94); Ting-Toomey and Kurogi (1998); Gutting (2016, pp. 49–51); Moll (2012, pp. 85–88)

Factor	Low-Context Culture	High-Context Culture
Locus of control and attribution for failure	Outer locus of control and blame of others for failure	Inner locus of control and personal acceptance for failure
Working/management style	Deal oriented: get down to business; work has value	Relationship oriented: first make friends then business; work is a necessity
Use of non-verbal communication	More focus on verbal communication than body language	Much nonverbal communication
Expression of reaction	Visible, external, outward reaction	Reserved, inward reactions
Values and norms	Independence, confrontation accepted	Conformity, harmony
Cohesion, family and friends	Flexible and open grouping patterns, changing as needed; value youth; little sense of loyalty	Strong distinction between in group and out group, Strong sense of family; value age; high sense of loyalty

Table 1: Communication factors in high- and low-context cultures[6]

1.1.2 Space

Halls explanation about cultural differences in the use of space formed the basis for the proxemics approach in cultural studies. Proxemics means the reference of space in human behavior or as Hall describes it: "[...] *the study of how men unconsciously structure microspace: The distance between men in the conduct of daily transactions, the organization of space in his houses and buildings and, ultimately the layout of his towns.*"[7] Hall distinguishes between *personal space* and *territory*. *Personal space* is the invisible circle surrounding a person, which may not be entered by someone else without permission. It varies depending on one's relationship to the people, the emotional state, cultural background, and the activity being performed. *Territoriality* is an innate characteristic. It describes the act of laying claim to and defending a specific territory. An example are cultures where people tend to establish places that they label "mine." Space can also communicate power and is perceived by all senses (auditory-, thermal-, kinesthetic-, and olfactory space). Spatial differences can give tone to communication, accent it, and even override the spoken word. As people interact,

[6] Based on Hollensen (2007, p. 220); Berger and Hagemann (2011, p. 17)
[7] Hall (1963, p. 1003)

the flow and shift of distance between them is integral to the communication process. People of close societies have little need for personal space and much lower territoriality. The opposite counts for far societies.[8]

1.1.3 Time

In his explanations, Hall distinguishes between *polychronic* and *monochronic* orientations of time. The *monochronic* concept follows the notion of handling tasks sequentially (one at a time). Time is experienced and used in a linear way, divided quite naturally into segments, scheduled and compartmentalized. It is used as a classification system for organizing life and setting priorities. Basically, time is used as a tool to prioritize tasks. One's schedule may take priority above everything else. Time is perceived as being almost tangible. Thus, it can be spent, saved, wasted and lost. *Polychronic* systems are the absolute antithesis of that: They follow the notion of handling multiple tasks at a time, subordinate to interpersonal relations. There is more emphasis on completing human transactions than on holding to schedules. Time is experienced as much less tangible. In addition, Hall describes a strong relation in cultures between time and space: In monochromic cultures, the emphasis is on the compartmentalization of functions and people (e.g. private offices are sound-proof). *Polychronic* people feel that separated offices disrupt the flow of communication by shutting people off from each other.[9]

Monochronic People	Polychronic People
- Do one thing at a time concentrate on the job. - Take time commitments (deadlines, schedules) seriously. - Are Low-Context and need information. - Are committed to the job. - Adhere religiously to plans. - Are concerned about not disturbing others; follow rules of privacy and consideration. - Show great respect for private property; seldom borrow or lend.	- Do many things at once. - Are Highly distractible and subject to interruptions. - Consider time commitments an objective to be achieved, if possible. - Are high-context and already have information. - Are committed to people and human relationships. - Change plans often and easily. - Are more concerned with those who are closely related (family, friends,

[8] Cf. Hall (1969, 1973), Dumetz (2012); Hall and Reed Hall (2001, p. 29); Rothlauf (2014, pp. 34–35); Müller and Gelbrich (2013, pp. 18–26); Gutting (2016, p. 48)
[9] Cf. Hall and Reed Hall (2001, pp. 31–33); Berger and Hagemann (2011, p. 18); Hall (1969, 1973), Dumetz (2012); Hall and Reed Hall (1990, pp. 12–22); Gutting (2016, pp. 51–52)

Monochronic People	Polychronic People
- Emphasize promptness. - Are accustomed to short-term relationships.	close business associates) than with privacy. - Borrow and lend things often and easily. - Base promptness on the relationship. - Have strong tendency to build lifetime relationships.

Table 2: Differences between monochronic and polychronic cultures[10]

1.2   Comparing U.S. and French Business Culture

The size of the United States as well as the ethnic and regional diversity of its population make it difficult to generalize about Americans.[11] While the country has absorbed millions of people from cultures around the globe, the core has its roots in northern European or Anglo-Saxon culture. Thus, to succeed in the American economic system, people must adapt to schedules and other conventions of doing business in a monochromic, low-context environment.[12]

In contrast, the French are predominantly polychronic and high-context. France has absorbed, albeit gradually, thousands of people from North Africa and other Mediterranean areas, which had a massive impact on its society. There are many regional differences and distinct subcultures within France, each with its own character and personality. In general, those people living in Paris and in the north, are more like other northern Europeans – formal, with greater personal distance – than residents of southern France, who have mainly Mediterranean influences. Again, these explanations underline the caution one should have by judging about individuals. The United States and France are examples par excellence how diverse cultures, even within a country, can be.[13]

1.2.1   Context in the U.S. and France

The American LC culture is defined by the tendency to communicate explicitly and directly. Society is task-centered (monochromic) and its primary purpose of

---

[10] Adopted from Hall and Reed Hall (1990, p. 15)
[11] Within the further explanations, the term *American(s)* will be used synonymously with *U.S.-citizens,* to ensure a fluent reading.
[12] Cf. Hall and Reed Hall (1990, pp. 139–140); Haller and Nägele (2013, pp. 125–129); Rentzsch (1999, pp. 212–213)
[13] Cf. Hall and Reed Hall (1990, pp. 87–92); WorldBusinessCulture.com ; eDiplomat (2015b); Haller and Nägele (2013, pp. 94–99); Rentzsch (1999, p. 176)

communication is to exchange information, facts, and opinions. Straight talking and directness are the norm. Arguments need to be supported with facts and figures to aid the decision-making process. Logic and linear thinking is being valued and people are expected to speak clearly in a straightforward manner. Thinking tends to be analytical, concepts are abstracted quickly, and the universal rule is preferred. Americans don't hesitate to criticize others in public. Their direct style of speech may be interpreted by foreigners as rude and cause embarrassment in other cultures. Especially people from HC cultures, as the French, see the desire of Americans to debate issues directly as aggressive and rude. In contrast, in the U.S., coded speech and verbosity is often seen as time wasting. Americans don't feel comfortable with indirectness and tend to miss nonverbal cues as a sign of a build-up tension in people. They are not ashamed to admit what they don't know and will assume a person understands something, if he or she doesn't tell the opposite. Thus, it is always proper for Americans to ask questions. They are very open in conversations about private affairs and will often ask personal questions, which may be perceived as intrusive by foreigners. An American company is an entity and exists independently from its employees. Hence, business relationships are formed between companies rather than between people. A personal contact is usually no requirement for establishing a long and successful business partnership. Having done so might not necessarily secure a deal over a rival, as Americans tend to strive for the best deal possible. Even the relationship between employer and employee is purely rational. Accountability within the company tends to be vertical and easily observable, as Americans like to know exactly what their responsibilities are and to whom they report. Their management style can be described as individualistic in approach, insofar as mangers are accountable for decisions made within their areas of responsibility. Technology is increasingly relied on and email is the normal methodology of communication. Email messages are expected to be short and to the point. This is just a quick and efficient approach resulting out of the LC culture and not meant as rudeness. Americans will use the telephone to conduct business that would require face-to-face meetings in other countries.[14]

French is known as one of the most beautiful languages in the world, as it outlines problems or conflicts in a very elegant way. The French are eloquent, relish conversation, and might perceive a direct communication as being frank. The way something is said is almost as important as what has been said. French indulge in small talk and like a little mystery in their dialogue. In general conversation they admire sophistication, erudition, nuance, and prefer subtlety and tact to frankness and fact. They will often talk around the point, as the listener is expected to understand the hidden message intuitively. However, the French do relish conflict and spirited discussions but rhetoric must be logical and well presented. Because they are highly contexed, the French expect other people to be similarly well informed. Thus, they don't give others much information. It is essential to maintain proper relationships with business partners and develop informal communications channels. One of the best ways for the French to get to know business partners, is to meet away from the office in pleasant surroundings, e.g. for lunch or dinner. Business may be discussed on occasion but never at the beginning of the meal. One should allow the French to take the initiative and they will glide into the topic at hand deftly with charm and elegance. They find it jarring when Americans insist on getting right to the point. In France, everything hinges on the salespeople's (long-term) relationship to the customer, which cannot be developed overnight. The French dichotomize their business and private life, keeping both totally separate. Socializing with professional colleagues is within the context of business and does not include one's family or private life. It is not considered polite to ask personal questions. One should beware of the superiors seeming informality at office parties: The French boss may appear relaxed on social occasions, which has misled unsuspecting Americans to lapse from formal politeness. A French boss can do so, but subordinates may not. Business people tend to be formal and conservative. Relationships are proper, orderly, and professional. The French share specialized information only within their own

---

[14] SRH FernHochschule (2014, pp. 43–49); Hall and Reed Hall (1990, pp. 144–149); eDiplomat (2015a); Haller and Nägele (2013, pp. 129–134); Hodge (2000, pp. 45–75); Rentzsch (1999, pp. 212–213)

network, which doesn't necessarily include subordinates. Foreigners tend to perceive the retention of information as an example of French arrogance and interpret it as a power play. Because they are both, high-context and polychronic, French expect everyone to know how to do everything properly. Thus, they tend to be autocratic in their business dealings. They won't tell subordinates or colleagues anything and get irritated if co-workers don't do something right. Such an attitude can be infuriating to foreign colleagues, particularly Americans. In decision-making both cultures, Americans and French, need facts and figures, however, they define and use data in different ways: Americans are primarily interested in the "bottom line," French are preoccupied with patterns and insist on synthesizing all data themselves. Everything about French meetings is different from American ones: tempo, style, and duration. The goal of a French meeting is to asses, brief, inform, be informed, feel out people's reactions, and encourage expression of opinions. French meetings have a fast tempo with prolonged discussions. Ideas are presented and elaborated upon, sometimes in philosophical terms, which is why meetings may last several hours without any definite agreement. When French attend American meetings, they are apt to feel shut out or restrained by the agenda and rigid adherence to schedules. This leads to frustration to the French participants, who are likely to want time for items not on the agenda.[15]

1.2.2 Space in the U.S. and France

Americans place high value on individuality and personal privacy. The monochromic, low-context behavior accompanies that businesspeople prefer private offices instead of working together in large open spaces. They avoid close physical contact and keep distance when conversing, automatically adjusting their chairs to a comfortable range. Generally, Americans tend to require more personal space than other cultures. If someone tries to get too close during a conversation, the counterpart will try to back away. During conversation, they maintain eye contact while listening but shift their view away when they speak. Americans gesture only moderately with their hands and arms, but their faces

---

[15] Cf. Hall and Reed Hall (1990, pp. 96–124); eDiplomat (2015b); WorldBusinessCulture.com (2017a); WorldBusinessCulture.com (2017b); Haller and Nägele (2013, pp. 99–102); Zeldin (1997, 161–394); Hodge (2000, pp. 72–73); Rentzsch (1999, pp. 176–178)

tend to be quite animated. They smile a lot in greetings and during formal introductions. It's common to shake hands, however, they do not with co-workers at the office every day. In social situations, some Americans shake hands; others hug or kiss friends of the opposite sex as a way of greeting; women often embrace; and men sometimes clap each other on the back. Most Americans do not touch other people, unless they are friends or relatives. They are generally uncomfortable with same-sex touching, especially between males.[16]

French space reflects their culture and institutions. Everything is centralized, and spatially the entire country is laid out around centers with Paris as the most important hub. Even French authority is highly centralized: The person in the center of any organization or any office is the person in control. Thus, in decision making, the French can move rapidly, because the centralized authority structure pairs with strong information networks – both typical for HC cultures. The French are high on the polychronic scale, which also reflects to their use of space, as it means they do many things at once. They can tolerate constant interruptions and are totally involved with people; maintain direct eye contact and use visual, auditory, and olfactory senses. French love to talk and communicate with their whole body, as well as with the spoken language. Their faces and gestures are very expressive, which reflects the intensity of their involvement with each other. The French stand and sit closer to each other than most Americans. In their interactions, they are totally engrossed and intent on their discussions. When friends meet, they shake hands or embrace, gesture, and maintain intense eye contact that enables them to read the other person's responses. In business dealings, however, they are more formal and restrained.[17]

1.2.3 Time in the U.S. and France

Most Americans are monochromic, especially in business. That means their time is scheduled and compartmentalized. Schedules are sacred and time commitments are taken very seriously. Americans like to do one thing after the other. Being on time is a very important rule of business etiquette. Regularly arriving late or missing appointments would have a negative impact on one's

---

[16] Cf. eDiplomat (2015a); SRH FernHochschule (2014, p. 52); Hall and Reed Hall (1990, pp. 143–151); *Haller/Nägele* (2013), S. 129–134; Hodge (2000, pp. 72–73)
[17] Cf. Hall and Reed Hall (1990, pp. 91–114); eDiplomat (2015b); WorldBusinessCulture.com (2017c); Haller and Nägele (2013, pp. 94–99); Hodge (2000, pp. 72–73)

business. Americans value a certain orderliness and don't like interruptions. Their consciousness is fixed in the present. They don't want to wait and become anxious when decisions are not made promptly. Monochromic people, as the Americans, tend to show a great deal of respect for private property and are reluctant to be either a lender or a borrower. This is part of a general tendency to follow rules of privacy and consideration as well as adhere to plans religiously. Promptness is sacred, especially where business appointments are concerned. American planning intervals are shorter than in many other countries. Since most American companies are publicly owned and must report all financial details quarterly, businesspeople tend to think in short-term intervals. When Americans talk about the "long term," they usually mean less than two or three years.[18]

French perception and handling of time is very different from the Americans. The French don't always adhere to schedules or appointments. In a polychronic system many interruptions and emergencies might occur. Like all polychronic people the French have elaborated information networks which must be maintained scrupulously to function effectively. These provide individuals with a constant update on the changing economic or political conditions that vitally affect their business. New information may require changing plans. What may appear to be a capricious change of mind to foreigners, is often a sensible adjustment to new environmental conditions. Hence, long-term planning is also difficult for the French. They are too aware of the many things that may prevent them from keeping a commitment. Another factor that affects French handling of time is the importance of *savoir-vivre:* The French insist on enjoying life now, making the most of each day. This includes living with a certain style and elegance, which is far more important than being a slave to some abstract idea of deadlines or schedules. Thus, French deadlines have an elastic quality to allow for life's uncertainties.[19]

---

[18] Cf. SRH FernHochschule (2014, pp. 42–48); Hall and Reed Hall (1990, pp. 139–146); *Haller/Nägele* (2013), S. 129–134; Hodge (2000, pp. 65–73)
[19] Cf. Hall and Reed Hall (1990, pp. 88–122); Hodge (2000, pp. 72–73); Rentzsch (1999, pp. 177–178)

2. Economy and Business in Turkey

2.1 Economy of Turkey – Introduction

The *Republic of Turkey* has made an impressive development since its founding in 1923. From being an economically backward country dominated by agriculture, Turkey's largely free-market economy is increasingly driven by its industry and service sectors nowadays.[20] Turkey is located at a proximity to Europe, Middle East and the Caucasus. It benefits from its location as a bridge between Europe and Asia, moreover it acts as an energy corridor connecting these two continents. The country offers an accessible, skilled workforce - the fourth largest labor force amongst EU members and accession countries. It boasts a large population of over 74 million people with an average age of 29, which is over a decade lower than the EU figure. Turkey's largely free-market economy is among the world's leading producer of agricultural products; textiles; construction materials; consumer electronics; home appliances motor vehicles, ships and other transportation equipment. The country is a founding member of the OECD (1961) and the G-20 major economies (1999).[21] While the *CIA* classifies Turkey as a development country, *The World Bank* ranks it as *an upper-middle income country* in terms of the country's per capita GDP. *Merrill Lynch, The World Bank*, and *The Economist* rate it as an *emerging market economy*. It scores 63.2 of 100 points and is ranked 70 on the *Economic Freedom Index*. Researchers state that Turkey's macroeconomic fundamentals are in a dynamic relationship with exchange market pressure. According to a survey by *Forbes* magazine, Istanbul, Turkey's financial capital, had a total of 37 billionaires in 2013, ranking 5th in the world behind Moscow, New York, Hong Kong and London.[22]

2.2 Economic Development and Economic Situation

In the late 19th and early 20th century, the Ottoman Empire's economy has been dominated by European forces. Trade agreements promoted the European merchants partially and the Empire had to commit parts of its means of income

---

[20] Cf. Central Intelligence Agency (2017); Finkel (2012, p. 50)
[21] Cf. International Monetary Fund (2017); Central Intelligence Agency (2017); PwC Turkey (2011)
[22] Cf. Investment Support and Promotion Agency of Turkey (2017d); Xiuqiong and Jinfa (2009); The Economist (2009); The World Bank (2017); OECD (2017b); Geromel (2013); Katırcıoğlu and Feridun (2011); The Heritage Foundation (2017); Central Intelligence Agency (2017)

to an international debt management. Against this background it becomes clear, that the founders of the Turkish Republic made economic independency one of their main targets. The *"All-Turkish Economy-Congress"* of 1923 supported an economic policy that, amongst others, targeted the development of a Turkish bourgeoisie, meaning a free enterprise system. Between 1923 and 1929 the country's economy recovered from its damages of WWI, however, an economic crisis in the early 1930's forced the government to a reformation of its economic system. Hence, statism (one of the six principles of Kemalism) has been integrated in the country's constitution with the country's industrialization as one of its main goals. The success of these new regulations has been lost during WWII.[23]

Triggered by the introduction of a multiple party system, Turkeys economic structure changed substantially in 1946. With the election of the *DP (Democratic Party)*, mainly interests of the country's agricultural population were represented. Agriculture has been promoted massively to increase exports. After an initial economic success, this policy led to a large trade deficit, whereby import restrictions had to be introduced. The policy of DP finally failed by high inflation rates and loss of real income for its bureaucrats and military officers. It had been ended by a military coup in 1960, which also increased the military's in politics and economy. In the 1960s and 70s a policy of import substitutions has been focused. Its goal was to increase the local production for goods that had consumed the Turkish forex. A short-term success wasn't sustainable, as the production of machines and primary products couldn't be fully executed inland. This situation led Turkey to another large economic crisis in 1979/80. As a reaction, the focus of the economic policy changed back to exports. The government supported exporting companies with subsidies, tax reductions and facilitations to import necessary input-goods. Exports and trade volume gained strongly. Certainly, this policy went to the disadvantage of workers and farmers: All unions, except the pro-government TÜRK-İŞ, were prohibited. Workers lost their right to strike and had to tolerate massive losses in real income. Indeed,

---

[23] Cf. Schuß (2012, pp. 328–333); Sansal (2016); Hershlag (1968, pp. 18–57); Schuß (2012, pp. 331–332); Finkel (2012, pp. 50–51); Berndt (2015, 106-107); Altunisik and Tür (2004, pp. 68–69)

inflation had been reduced in short-term until the end of the 1980's. In this not completely stabilized environment, the Turkish government fully liberalized the country's capital market.[24]

The years 1990 to 2001 have been strongly influenced by a cyclic economic development with alternated years of high growth rates and strong economic crises. Reasons can be found in structural weaknesses of several institutional departments as well as the mainly short-term focused, populistic economic policy of the several governments during this period. By the end of the 1980s, the former government lifted the ban on political parties, unions and strikes. Thus, the position of workers and farmers improved. The reduction of import barriers led to a higher pressure of competition for Turkish businesses. The peak of this development had been reached in 1996, with Turkey entering the European Customs Union. Economic experts feared an economical break down which didn't appear but the expected increase of FDI's also held off. Altogether, in the years from 1990 the Turkish economy grew around 5% anually, although it experienced several economic crises. The country's last crisis in 2001 included one of the highest recessions in Turkish history (8% decrease in economic performance). It had been introduced by the country's large trade deficit resulting out of the macro-economic problems, which forced the country's central bank to deregulate Turkish Lira. The currency lost around 40% of its value within a few hours, whereby foreign debt increased dramatically and led to an excessive governments indebtedness, as well as the bankruptcy of many private businesses. 21 banks went bankrupt. To avoid the country's bankruptcy, the IMF granted a credit of USD 31 billion between 2002 and 2004.[25]

After this severe financial crisis, Ankara adopted financial and fiscal reforms as part of an IMF program. These strengthened the country's economic fundamentals and ushered in an era of strong growth. This development has additionally been supported by the conservative AKP party, which was able to govern the country solely and thus, establish a long-term orientated economic

---

[24] Cf. Schuß (2012, pp. 333–335); Ertuğrul and Selçuk (2001); Ari and Cergibozan (2016, pp. 124–126); Finkel (2012, pp. 51–56); Berndt (2015, pp. 107–109); Altunisik and Tür (2004, pp. 69–83)

[25] Cf. Schuß (2012, pp. 337–339); Ertuğrul and Selçuk (2001, pp. 6–27); Ari and Cergibozan (2016, pp. 124–126); Finkel (2012, pp. 51–56)

policy. It focused a financial recovery of the national budget and a comprehensive reformation of public institutions including an aggressive privatization program. Thereby the EU-criteria could be fulfilled insofar that, in October 2005, accession negotiations between Turkey and the EU officially started. This step gained additional trust of foreign investors. Thereby, not just foreign capital but also new FDIs began to flow into the country. An emerging cadre of middle-class entrepreneurs added dynamism to the economy. Global economic conditions and tighter fiscal policy caused the country's GDP to contract in 2009. Therefore, various economic stimulus measures were introduced, which could reduce the global crisis' impact. GDP rebounded strongly in 2010/11, as exports returned to a normal level. The Turkish stock market and credit rating agencies have responded positively. Two rating agencies upgraded Turkey's debt to investment grade in 2012 and 2013. The country has become an attractive destination for FDI. Majority of inflows primarily came from the EU, followed by North America and Asia. Despite these positive trends, GDP growth dropped to 4.4% in 2013 and 2.9% in 2014. Growth slowed considerably in the last quarter of 2014, largely due to lackluster consumer demand, both, domestically and in Europe - Turkey's most important export market. High interest rates have also contributed the slowdown in growth, as Turkey sharply increased interest rates in January 2014, to strengthen the country's currency and reduce inflation. The Turkish economy retains significant weaknesses, which will be discussed in *part 2.5*. However, the country still has the world's 18th-largest nominal GDP, and 17th-largest GDP by PPP. Following figures shows the development of the country's GDP and FDI inflows from 1960 to 2016. *Table 3* summarizes the country's economic data.[26]

---

[26] Cf. Carlson (2013); Butler (2012); Xie, Gokoluk, and Selcuk (2013); Kılınç, Kılınç, and Turhan (2012, pp. 19–32); The Economist (2010); Kardas (2009); Geromel (2013); Ari and Cergibozan (2016, pp. 124–126); Central Intelligence Agency (2017); Schuß (2012, pp. 339–356); Ari and Cergibozan (2016, pp. 124–126); Altunisik and Tür (2004, pp. 83–87); Finkel and Harvey (2014); Republic of Turkey Prime Ministry Investment Support and Promotion Agency (2014)

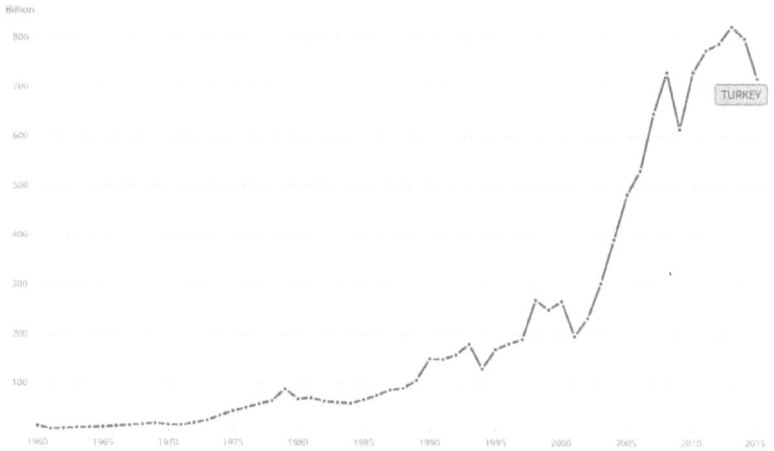

Figure 1: Growth Domestic Product - Turkey 1960-2015 (current USD)[27]

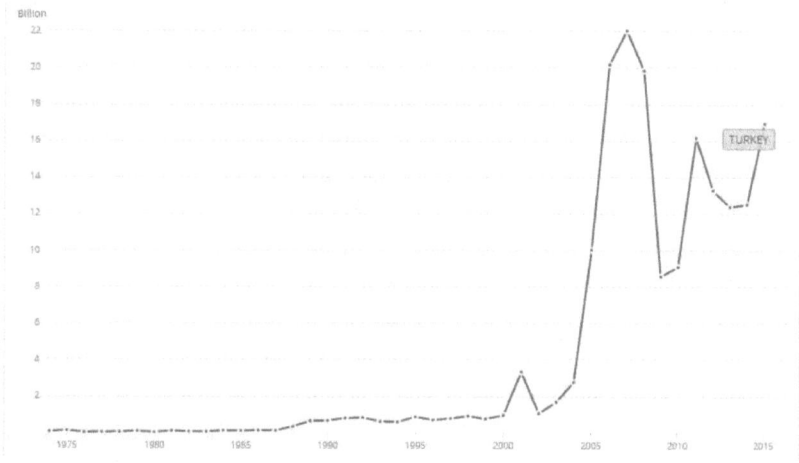

Figure 2: FDI, net Inflows, current USD, Turkey 1974 - 2015[28]

---

[27] Source: World Bank (2017)
[28] Source: World Bank (2017)

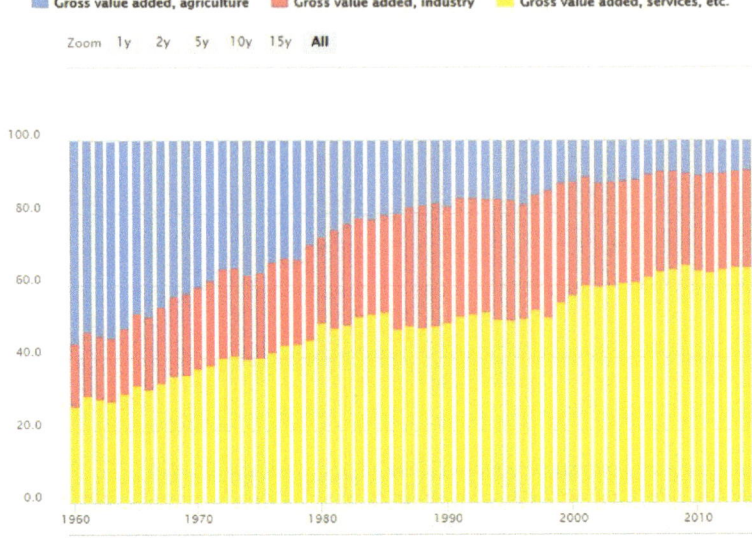

Figure 3: Structure of gross value added by sectors - Turkey[29]

The Turkish Republic in Figures	
Land Area	783,562.38 km²
Population	78.7 million (2015)
Population density	102/km2
Life expectancy	75.3 years
Adult literacy	
Household disposable income	16,870 USD / per capita
The Economy	
Currency	Turkish Lira (TRY)
GDP	USD 861 billion (2015-Current Prices)
GDP per capita (PPP)	$ 21,100 (2016 est.)
Unemployment rate:	2,8% (2016 est.)
Main Exports (Types)	apparel, foodstuffs, textiles, metal manufactures, transport equipment
Destinations (% total)	Germany (9.3%) UK (7.3%) Iraq (5.9%) Italy (4.8%) USA (4.4%) France (4.1%) Switzerland (3.9%) Spain (3.3%) UAE (3.3%)

[29] Source: Bluenomics (2017)

	Iran (2.5%) (2015)
Main Imports (type)	machinery, chemicals, semi-finished goods, fuels, transport equipment
Major Imports (sources)	China (12%); Germany (10.3%); Russia (9.8%); USA (5.4%); Italy (5.1%); France (3.7%); South Korea (3.4%); Iran (2.9%); India (2.7%); Spain (2.7%) (2015)
Natural Resources	coal, iron ore, copper, chromium, antimony, mercury, gold, barite, borate, celestite (strontium), emery, feldspar, limestone, magnesite, marble, perlite, pumice, pyrites (sulfur), clay, arable land, hydropower
Trade Agreements	Part of the EU customs agreement Free trade agreements with: Albania, Bosnia Herzegovina, Chile, Croatia, EFTA member countries (Switzerland, Norway, Iceland and Liechtenstein), Egypt, Georgia, Israel, Jordan, South Korea, Macedonia, Malaysia, Mauritius, Montenegro, Morocco, Palestine, Serbia, Tunisia

Table 3: The Turkish Republic in Figures (Profile)[30]

2.3 Major Industries and Important Companies

2.3.1 Agriculture

Turkey's agricultural sector is world famous for its production of hazelnuts, cherries, figs, apricots, quinces, pomegranates, watermelons, cucumbers, chickpeas, tomatoes, eggplants, green pepper, lentils, pistachios, onions, olives, sugar beet, tobacco, tea, apples, cotton, barley, almonds, wheat, rye, grapefruit and lemons. Turkey has been self-sufficient in food production since the 1980s. Agriculture still accounts for about 25% of employment. Fruit and vegetables from

---

[30] Adopted from Central Intelligence Agency (2017); OECD (2017a); Investment Support and Promotion Agency of Turkey (2017d)

Turkey were exported to the EU worth € 738.4 million up to September 2016 - an increase of 21% compared to the same period in 2015. Turkey is the EU's fourth largest vegetable supplier and the seventh largest fruit supplier. The country has USD 150 billion gross agricultural domestic product in total, USD 40 billion agricultural exports.[31]

2.3.2 Industrial Sector

Turkey's industrial sector is dominated by private industrialist families like *Sabancı* and *Koç*. Manufacturing is the country's main industrial activity with textiles and automobiles as the leading sectors. It comprises 27% of GDP and employs nearly 28% of the workforce.[32]

Consumer Electronics

Electronics sector in Turkey represents 2% of the total GDP. The growing electronics industry allows Turkey to channel strong FDI inflows into the country. In 2011, Turkey's electronics sector received USD 442 million of FDI inflow. In 2012, Turkish electronics production increased by 4.1% reaching USD 12.4 billion, whereas exports increased by 5.2%, reaching USD 6.8 billion. Turkish manufacturing companies *Vestel, Beko* or *Profilo-Telra* produce TVs for almost every famous brand manufacturer. Two thirds of the produced goods are being exported to the EU. Furthermore, the production of white goods gains importance. Companies like *Robert Bosch GmbH* and *Sony* own manufacturing plants in Turkey.[33]

Textiles and clothing

Textiles and clothing are the most important sectors of the Turkish economy with the biggest export quota. Accounting for about 7% of the GDP, these two sectors are the core of Turkish economy in terms of GDP contribution, share in manufacturing, employment, investments and macroeconomic indicators. These sectors had a 10.32% share (14.842 billion USD) in total export volume in 2015. Textile and clothing production benefit from Turkey's position as the 6th biggest cotton producer in the world. The textiles industry tries to differentiate itself from

---

[31] Cf. Investment Support and Promotion Agency of Turkey (2017a); Fresh Plaza (2016); Central Intelligence Agency (2017); Investment Support and Promotion Agency of Turkey (2017a)
[32] Cf. Nordea Trade (2017); Berndt (2015, pp. 112–113)
[33] Cf. Republic of Turkey Prime Ministry Investment Support and Promotion Agency (2014); PwC Turkey (2011); Berndt (2015, p. 114)

China increasing the production of branded articles instead of cheap mass products.[34]

Motor vehicles and automotive products

13 OEM manufacturers which produce over 1 million vehicles yearly, making Turkey the 16th biggest automotive manufacturer in the world. OEMs include *MAN, Daimler AG, Toyota, Renault, Fiat, Hyundai* and *Ford*. According to industry group the Automotive Manufacturers Association, production grew 9% annually to 1.14 million units in 2016. Nearly 80% of vehicles produced in Turkey were exported.[35]

Machinery

Turkey's machinery production value accounts for 2.4% of nominal GDP with a capacity utilization of 73% (2011). In 2012, Turkey exported USD 21 billion worth of machinery. FDI inflow for machinery manufacturing increased from USD 26 million to USD 513 million with a CAGR of 64%.[36]

2.3.3 Services

Transportation and Logistics

In 2013, there were 98 airports in Turkey including 22 international airports. As of 2015, *Istanbul Atatürk Airport* is the 11th busiest airport in the world, serving 31,833,324 passengers between January and July 2014, according to *Airports Council International*. The new, third international airport of Istanbul is planned to be the largest airport in the world, with a capacity to serve 150 million passengers per year. *Turkish Airlines*, flag carrier of Turkey, was selected by *Skytrax* as Europe's best airline for five consecutive years from 2011 and 2015. Turkey's current logistics industry size is estimated to be USD 80-100 billion and is forecast to reach USD 108-140 billion by 2017.[37]

Tourism

Turkey is currently the 6th most popular tourist destination in the world, attracting more than 30 million tourists annually. Tourism is one of the most dynamic

---

[34] Cf. Republic of Turkey. Ministry of Economy. (2016); PwC Turkey (2011); Berndt (2015, pp. 112–113)

[35] Cf. Sano (2017); Berndt (2015, p. 113); Investment Support and Promotion Agency Turkey (2014); PwC Turkey (2011)

[36] Cf. Investment Support and Promotion Agency of Turkey (2014)

[37] Cf. Investment Support and Promotion Agency of Turkey (2013); Airports Council International (2015); Sharkov (2014); Mezzofiore (2014)

industries in Turkey. According to the *Ministry of Culture and Tourism*, the number of foreign travelers arriving in Turkey in 2015 was 39.4 million, while total turnover of the tourism industry that same year was USD 31.4 billion. Growth in the Turkish tourism industry has been above the global average in recent years. The direct contribution of the industry to the current account deficit in 2015 was 8%, while its contribution to GDP reached 4.37 % the same year.[38]

2.3.4 Major Companies

In 2016, eleven Turkish companies were listed in the *Forbes Global 2000* list - an annual ranking of the top 2000 public companies in the world.[39]

World Rank	Company	Industry	Revenue	Profits	Assets	Market Value
#447	Isbank	Banking	14.6	1.8	114.5	7.8
#451	Koç Holding	Conglomerate	25.5	1.3	25.1	13.5
#482	Garanti Bank	Banking	8.3	1.4	94.2	12.5
#534	Akbank	Banking	7.1	1.2	86	12
#619	Sabancı Holding	Conglomerate	11.4	0.787	91.2	7.3
#878	Halkbank	Banking	6.3	1	66.7	4.8
#947	VakifBank	Banking	6.2	0.719	66.9	4.5
#971	Turkish Airlines	Transportation	10.5	1.1	16.3	3.4
#1292	Turkcell	Communication	4.7	0.753	9.1	9.3
#1455	Turk Telekom	Communication	5.2	0.453	9.9	8.2
#1630	Enka	Construction Services	4.5	0.528	7.1	7

Table 4: Turkey's biggest Companies in 2015 (billion USD)[40]

It has been mentioned, that Turkeys industrial sector is dominated by private industrialist families like *Sabancı* and *Koç*, which will be described in the table below.[41]

Sabancı Holding   The Sabancı family is one of the richest Turkish industrial families. 78% of the holding company are still family-owned. It controls around 65 companies. Known for the modern Istanbul are the Sabancı Twin Towers, a prestige building at the beginning of Istanbul's business district Levent in the Beşiktaş

---

[38] Cf. Investment Support and Promotion Agency of Turkey (2017c); PwC Turkey (2011)
[39] Cf. Forbes Magazine (2016)
[40] Source: Forbes Magazine (2016)
[41] Cf. Nordea Trade (2017); Berndt (2015, pp. 112–113)

area. Company founder Ömer Sabancı (1906-1966) started its career in cotton trade and expanded in other industrial sectors. His son Sakip Sabancı (1933-2004) was one of the biggest art collectors in Turkey and owned a meaningful collection of Ottoman calligraphy. Nowadays the nice of the company's founder, Güler Sabancı, leads the holding as its chief executive.[42]
Koç Holding   Koç Holding is a Turkish business group with over 90.000 employees worldwide. It's the only Turkish company in the Fortune Global 500 list and it stands for 12% of the country's total export volume. Koç Holding is one of the 50 biggest companies outside the U.S. Their businesses produce cars, white goods and groceries. Further business segments are energy, information technology, tourism and constructions. A big part of the businesses is being leaded with foreign companies as Ford.   Koç Holding was founded in the 1920s by Vehbi Koç. Between 1984 – 2003 it has been leaded by his son, Rahmi Koç who passed leadership to his son Mustafa.   The family engages in social and cultural fields. The Vehbi- Koç-Foundation aliments a University, several schools and the Rahmi-M.- Koç-Museum in Istanbul. The *Vehbi Koç National Park* is located the entrance of the Fatih-Sultan-Mehmet-Bridge in Beykoz.[43]

Table 5: Important private holdings in Turkey

2.4 Foreign Trade

Turkish business executives and government officials believe the quickest route to achieving export growth lies outside traditional western markets. According to *Daniel Dombey* of the *Financial Times "[...] [the] European Union accounted for much more than half of all Turkey's exports. Now the figure is heading down toward not much more than a third."*[44] Erdem Başçı, Turkey's central bank governor, predicts that *Iraq* will eventually become Turkey's largest export market. The Turkish government is intricately involved in helping to facilitate private sector expansion in emerging markets. *Hüsnü Özyeğin*, one of Turkey's most prominent businessmen and bankers, states that the country's government strategy is to open more embassies in growth regions and emerging markets. *Turkish Airlines* will target these regions to enable businessmen to travel and evolve business there. Similarly, *Ahmet Davutoğlu*, Turkey's prime minister, is focusing his attentions on the Middle East and striking a series of visa-free travel deals, while eyeing to establish free trade zones with countries in that region. The

---

[42] Cf. Schuß (2012, p. 332); Sabancı Holding (2017)
[43] Cf. Schuß (2012, p. 363); Koç Holding (2017)
[44] Dombey (2013b)

AKP government is also seeking to improve economic and political relations with the autonomous Kurdish Regional Government in northern Iraq.[45]

Turkey has been a member of the *World Trade Organization* since 1995. The country's commitment to integrating regional and international trade norms can be seen in its participation in and membership of various organizations including the *Economic Cooperation Organization, United Nations Conference on Trade and Development, Organization of the Black Sea Economic Cooperation, World Customs Organization, International Chamber of Commerce, D-8*, and various other organizations.[46] Major import and export markets have been mentioned in *Table 3: The Turkish Republic in Figures (Profile)*. Following table ranks major export product groups.

	Product Groups	USD billion	Share in total exports (%)
1	Vehicles other than railway or tramway rolling-stock, parts thereof	19.804	13.9
2	Boilers, machineries and mechanical appliances, parts thereof	12.405	8.7
3	Precious stones, precious metals, pearls and articles thereof	12.176	8.5
4	Knitted and crocheted goods, and articles thereof	8.855	6.2
5	Electrical machinery and equipment, parts thereof	7.778	5.5
6	Iron and steel	6.187	4.3
7	Non-knitted and crocheted goods, and articles thereof	5.928	4.2
8	Plastic and articles thereof	5.027	3.5
9	Articles of iron and steel	4.967	3.5
10	Edible fruits and nuts, peel of melons or citrus fruits	3.873	2.7

Table 6: Top 10 Export Product Groups in 2016[47]

---

[45] Cf. Dombey (2013a); Dombey (2013b)
[46] Cf. Investment Support and Promotion Agency of Turkey (2017b)
[47] Adopted from Workman (2017); Investment Support and Promotion Agency of Turkey (2017b)

2.5 Current Challenges

Turkey is still experiencing large structural problems. The area of Istanbul is reaching 41% of the average income of the 15 "old" EU-states, while the country's east just 7%. Several projects have been introduced to develop the eastern part of the country. Other macro-economic, structural problems can be seen, e.g. while the agricultural sector is employing 30.6% of labor, it only generates 11.9% of the country's GDP.[48]

After years of enormous economic growth, the figure for the third quarter of 2016 is likely to be negative and around 0.5%. The Turkish economy is contracting for the first time since mid-2009. Its manufacturing industry continued to shrink for a third quarter in a row with contraction reaching nearly 5% in the third quarter. The construction sector also plunged into recession in the third quarter, shrinking around 5%. Agricultural and service sectors had contracted by about 1% and 2%, respectively, since the beginning of 2016.[49]

From 2015 and continuing in 2016, Turkey witnessed an uptick in terrorist violence. On July 15th, 2016, elements of the Turkish armed forces attempted a coup at key government and infrastructure locations in Ankara and Istanbul. An estimated of 300 people were killed and over 2,000 injured. In response, Turkish government authorities arrested and/or dismissed thousands of military personnel, journalists, and civil servants with the attempted coup. Furthermore, it instituted a three-month state of emergency that was extended in October 2016. In a national referendum on April 14th, 2017, citizens of Turkey voted for changing the state to an executive presidency. Additionally, the subsequent security vacuum from the widespread purges, alongside Turkey's increased presence in Syria, have resulted in an ever-increasing number of attacks from IS and PKK militants, intensifying instability in the country's southeast. The country is suffering from a substantial decline in tourism (down by 40% from 2015) with the number of foreign arrivals dropping by more than 21%. This has had a substantial impact to its economy, with tourism contributing 12.9% of its GDP in 2015. Turkey's fragile security environment is only one of its growing concerns. The mentioned turbulence from the country's political volatilities following the

---

[48] Cf, Berndt (2015, pp. 117–119)
[49] Cf. Sonmez (2017)

attempted military coup have exposed its vulnerabilities to global capital flows with FDI departing the country at an unprecedented pace. Furthermore, the domestic saving rate, stagnant productivity, unemployment, and rapidly increasing labor costs, all adversely affect growth. These things need to be addressed by enacting substantial, long-overdue structural reforms that mostly are independent of security concerns.[50]

Altogether 2016 has been a difficult year for Turkey. The Turkish Lira lost 20% of its value and economic growth slowed down to 2.5%. In September 2016, rating agency *Moody's* cut Turkey's sovereign debt to junk status. In 2017, Turkey is likely to face in volatile growth rates, high-levels of international debt, and political fights over monetary policy.[51]

---

[50] Cf. Veldhuizen (2017); Unver (2016); Central Intelligence Agency (2017)
[51] Cf. Veldhuizen (2017); n-tv (2017)

3. The 7-D-Model for analyzing cultural differences

3.1 Hampden-Turner and Trompenaars' 7-D-Model

Based on *Hall's* and *Hofstede's* work, *Fons Trompenaars* and *Charles Hampden-Turner* developed their own theory for analyzing cultural differences. The researches assumed that humans had to succeed three basic sources of challenges:[52]

- Relationships between people (friends, employees, customers and bosses).
- Managing time and aging.
- Relationship to the environment (be it benign or threatening).

Cultures use different ways to deal with these problems. To explain how, the researchers derived seven dimensions from these basic sources, of which five answer the question of relationships between people, and respectively one the relationship to time and the environment:[53]

1. Universalism vs. particularism: What is more important, the rules or exceptions based on relationships?
2. Individualism vs. communitarianism: Do we function in a group or as individuals?
3. Neutral vs. affective: How do we express our emotions?
4. Specific vs. diffuse: How separate do we keep our private and working lives?
5. Achievement vs. ascription: Do we have to prove ourselves to receive status, or is it given to us?
6. Past, present, future: Do we focus on our heritage, the present day, or what will come tomorrow?
7. Internal vs. external control: Do we control our environment, or are we controlled by it?

In summary, the model looks at values which help to explain cultural differences in society and how those affect businesses. It provides a framework for identifying implicit values and norms that a society has developed to deal with the regular problems it faces. In principle, everyone in the world values both sides of each

---

[52] Cf. Rothlauf (2012, p. 52); Berger and Hagemann (2011, pp. 26–28); Trompenaars and Hampden-Turner (2012, p. 39); Gutting (2016, p. 52)
[53] Cf. Blom and Meier (2004, p. 56); Rothlauf (2012, p. 52); Berger and Hagemann (2011, pp. 26–28); Trompenaars and Hampden-Turner (2012, pp. 11–14); Trompenaars and Coebergh (2015, pp. 201–203)

dimension, but different groups of people approach a situation with a cultural preference. It is the tension between the extremes of the continuum that gives energy for the resolution or reconciliation of the cultural dilemma. Dilemmas are shared, while approaches are cultural. The next parts describe the seven dimensions with practical examples of daily business. These will express the difficulties leaders are confronted with when trying to integrate seemingly opposing values. What has already been mentioned in part one of this assignment shall be repeated at this point: cultural models should be used to gain sensibility about one's own culture and possible sources of conflict. One should be careful not to prejudice about individuals.[54]

3.1.1 Universalism versus Particularism

This dimension defines how people judge others behavior. It reflects the primacy of the "general" in opposition to the primacy of the "specific". While universalists particularly emphasize the compliance with rules or laws (rule-based behavior), particularists pay more attention to the circumstances or personal backgrounds, as they focus on the exceptional nature of present circumstances. [55] *„Businesspeople from both societies will tend to think each other corrupt. A universalist will say of particularists, 'They cannot be trusted, because they will always help their friends,' and a particularist, conversely, will say of universalists, 'You cannot trust them; they would not even help a friend.'"*[56]

The researchers demonstrate the difficulty to integrate opposing values in an example of a Swedish software company that had been acquired by an American enterprise. Three children of the company's founder were working for the company. The buying company was convinced that rewards for salespeople most reflect the increasing competition in the market and therefore decreed that a part of remuneration must depend on individual performance. As the co-founder of the company, the first son he earned a share of the acquisition payment. e had a good year privately but also businesswise, he easily reached his target and earned the bonus, which still was a small percentage of his total income. Due to

---

[54] Cf. Rothlauf (2012, p. 52); Berger and Hagemann (2011, pp. 26–28); Trompenaars and Hampden-Turner (2012)

[55] Cf. Rothlauf (2012, pp. 52–53); Trompenaars and Hampden-Turner (2012, pp. 41–43); Hodge (2000, pp. 55–60)

[56] Trompenaars and Hampden-Turner (2012, p. 42)

average sales figures, the income of the second son would be reduced. The founder's daughter has two children while her husband died in an air crash. This tragic event caused her to have a very weak sales year. While the founder believes that performance should be rewarded and favoritism should be avoided, he knows that unusual circumstances in the lives of his children have made this contest anything but fair. The rewards withheld will hurt more deeply than the rewards bestowed will motivate. His family later says they feel let down. Another example where the universalism-versus-particularism-dilemma shows up is the contract: Weighty contracts are common in universalist cultures. However, contracts with strict requirements and penalty clauses may imply the message that one party would cheat the other. One serious pitfall for universalist cultures in doing business with particularistic ones is that the importance of the relationship is often ignored. The contract will be seen as definitive by the universalist, but only as a rough guideline or approximation by the particularist. The latter will want to make the contract as vague as possible and may object to clauses that are restrictive. [57]

Universalism	Particularism
Differences	
- Focus is more on rules than on relationships.	- Focus is more on relationship than on rules.
- Legal contracts are readily drawn up.	- Legal contracts are readily modified.
- A trustworthy is the one who honors their work or contract.	- A trustworthy is the one who honors changing circumstances.
- There is only one truth or reality, that which has been agreed to.	- There are several perspectives on reality relative to each participant.
- A deal is a deal.	- Relationship evolves.
Tips for doing Business:	
- Be prepared for "rational," "professional" arguments and presentations that push for your acquiescence.	- Be prepared for personal "meandering" or "irrelevancies" that do not seem to be going anywhere.
- Do not take impersonal "get down to business" attitudes as rude.	- Do not take personal, "get to know you" attitudes as small talk.
- Carefully prepare the legal ground with a lawyer if in doubt.	- Carefully consider the personal implications of your legal "safeguards."
Managing and Being Managed:	

---

[57] Cf. Trompenaars and Hampden-Turner (2012, pp. 43–56); Gutting (2016, pp. 53–54);

Universalism	Particularism
- Strive for consistency and uniform procedures.	- Build informal networks and create private understandings.
- Institute formal ways of changing the way business is conducted.	- Try to alter informally accustomed patterns of activity.
- Modify the system so that the system will modify you.	- Modify relations with you so that you will modify the system.
- Signal changes publicly	- Pull levers privately.
- Seek fairness by treating all like cases in the same way.	- Seek fairness by treating all cases on their special merits.

Table 7: Universalism vs. Particularism[58]

3.1.2 Individualism versus Collectivism

The central question is whether individuals primarily see themselves as individuals or define themselves through the affiliation to a group. It's the question if an individual relates to others by discovering what he or she wants individually and then tries to negotiate the differences or does the individuum place some shared concept of the public and collective good ahead of others. International management is seriously affected by individualist-versus-communitarian preferences within various countries.[59]

An example for conflict potential between individualistic and collectivistic cultures can be found in an international enterprise that holds sales-meetings with representatives of their foreign subsidiaries: While collectivistic cultures tend to send a group of representatives or a representative with the most knowledge about the specific topic, individualistic cultures tend to send the same representative to every meeting (e.g. the head of sales). Another example can be seen in the translator: Individualistic cultures supposed him or her to be neutral while in communitarian cultures, he or she will usually serve the group, engaging members in lengthy asides and attempting to mediate misunderstandings. Often, he or she may be the top negotiator in the group.[60]

[58] Adopted from: Hoecklin (1998, p. 41); Trompenaars and Hampden-Turner (2012, pp. 62–63); Gutting (2016, pp. 53–54)
[59] Cf. Rothlauf (2012, p. 53); Trompenaars and Hampden-Turner (2012, pp. 65–67); Gutting (2016, pp. 55–56)
[60] Cf. Trompenaars and Hampden-Turner (2012, pp. 76–78); Gutting (2016, pp. 55–56)

Individualism	Collectivism/Communitarianism
Differences:	
- More frequent use of 'I' and 'me'. - In negotiations, decisions typically made on the spot by a representative. - People ideally achieve alone and assume personal responsibility. - Holidays taken in pairs or even alone.	- More frequent use of 'we'. - Decisions typically referred back by delegate to the organization. - People ideally achieve in groups which assume joint responsibility. - Holidays taken in organized groups, or with extended family.
Tips for doing Business	
- Prepare for quick decisions and sudden offers not referred to HQ. - A negotiator can commit those who sent him or her and is reluctant to go back on an undertaking. - The toughest negotiations were probably already done within the organization while preparing for the meeting. You have a tough job selling them the solution to this meeting. Conducting business alone means that this person is respected by his or her company and has its esteem. - The aim is to make a quick deal.	- Show patience for time taken to consent and to consult. - A negotiator can agree only tentatively and may withdraw an undertaking after consulting with superiors. - The toughest negotiations are with the communitarians you face. You must somehow persuade them to cede to you points that the multiple interests in your company demand. - Conducting business when surrounded by helpers means that this person has high status in his or her company. - The aim is to build lasting relationships
Managing and being Managed	
- Try to adjust individual needs to organizational needs. - Introduce methods of individual incentives such as pay-for-performance, individual assessment, and managing by objectives. - Expect job turnover and mobility to be high. - Seek out high performers, heroes and champions for special praise. - Give people the freedom to take initiative.	- Seek to integrate personality with authority within the group. - Give attention to esprit de corps, morale, and cohesiveness. - Have low job turnover and mobility. - Extol the whole group and avoid showing favoritism. - Hold up superordinate goals for all to meet.

Table 8: Individualism vs. Collectivism[61]

---

[61] Adopted from: Hoecklin (1998, p. 41); Trompenaars and Hampden-Turner (2012, pp. 98–99)

3.1.3 Neutral vs. Affective

The third dimension deals with the importance of feelings and relationships. In affective cultures, feelings and emotions are not restrained, whereas instrumentality and rationality of actions are the focus in neutral cultures. Simplified, one can say that one also differentiates between "impulsive behavior" and "disciplined behavior". However, one should be cautious in not overinterpreting such differences. Neutral cultures are not necessarily cold or unfeeling, nor are they emotionally constipated or repressed. The amount of emotion people show is often the result of convention. [62]

An example for a clash could be a meeting in which a new idea gets discussed. A Dutch representative within the meeting calls the idea of the Italians "crazy". Even before he had a chance to explain why he thought it was crazy, the Italian colleagues leave the room for a time-out. The Dutch complains about those "excitable" Italians. In some cultures, as the British and US culture, authors often start workshops with a cartoon or anecdote that makes a joke about the main points to be covered. This form of icebreaker is always a success. Hence, In Germany, these introductions don't seem to work that well. The audience tends to take notes and looks puzzled after the presenter tells the joke. However, there would be a lot of laughter in the bar and, eventually, even in the sessions. Simply, that levity was not permissible in a professional setting between strangers.[63]

A Spanish salesman with long-year experience as a sales manager in Arabic and Latin-American countries had been promoted to south-east Asia. His appearance was noisy, emotional and enthusiastic – characteristics that have been impressive in emotional/affective cultures. However, in the neutral, reserved Chinese culture he couldn't succeed. Customers avoided him or referred to difficulties in budget approvals. His company redeployed him to Sweden, another mistake. The cold, and fact-orientated Swedish had no appreciation for the lavish style of the salesmen.[64]

---

[62] Cf. Rothlauf (2012, pp. 54–55); Gutting (2016, p. 56);
[63] Cf. Hampden-Turner and Trompenaars (2000, pp. 89–96)
[64] Cf. Rentzsch (1999, pp. 37–38)

Neutral	Emotional/Affective
Differences	
- Opaque emotional state. - Do not readily express what they think and feel. - Embarrassed and awkward at public displays of emotions. - Discomfort with physical contact outside private cycle. - Subtle in verbal and non-verbal expressions.	- Show immediate reactions either verbally or non-verbally. - Expressive face and body signals. - At ease with physical contact. - Raise voice readily.
Tips for doing Business	
- Ask for time-outs from meetings and negotiations where you can patch each other up and rest between games of poker with the Impassive Ones. - Put as much as you can on paper beforehand. - Their lack of emotional tone does not mean they are disinterested or bored; it means only that they do not like to show their hand. - The entire negotiation is typically focused on the object or proposition being discussed, not so much on you personally.	- Do not be put off your stride when they create scenes and get histrionic; take time-outs for sober reflection and hard assessments. - When they are expressing goodwill, respond warmly. - Their enthusiasm, readiness to agree, or vehement disagreement does not mean that they have made up their minds. - The entire negotiation is typically focused on you personally, not so much on the object or proposition being discussed.
Managing and being Managed	
- Avoid warm, expressive, or enthusiastic behavior. Such behavior is interpreted as lack of control over your feelings and inconsistent with high status. - If you prepare extensively beforehand, you will find it easier to "stick to the point" – that is, to the neutral topics being discussed. - Look for subtle indications that the person is pleased or angry, and amplify their importance.	- Avoid detached, ambiguous, and cool demeanors. Such demeanors will be interpreted as negative evaluation, as disdain, dislike, and social distance. You are excluding them from "the family." - If you discover whose work, energy, and enthusiasm has been invested in which projects, you are more likely to appreciate tenacious positions. - Tolerate great "Surfeits" of emotionality without getting intimidated or coerced, and moderate their importance.

Table 9: Neutral vs. Emotional/Affective[65]

---

[65] Adopted from Hampden-Turner and Trompenaars (2000, pp. 98–99)

3.1.4 Specific vs. Diffuse

This dimension is in also called *"dimension of consternation/engagement"*, expressing an individual's degree of consternation in a certain situation or action. In diffuse cultures, the different areas of life cannot be separated from each other. In specific cultures, however, the areas of life are clearly differentiated (e.g. work and family). Trompenaars and Hampden-Turner state that specific cultures correlate with low-context cultures while diffuse cultures do with high-context-cultures. [66] The Italians which idea had been called „crazy" by their Dutch colleague feel like he questions their ability to do a proper job. While the Dutch guy was talking about the idea itself (specific), the Italians didn't separate the Idea from themselves (diffuse). Specific oriented cultures choose management by objectives and pay-for-performance as favorite devices to motivate employees. In MBO you first agree on the "objectives" – that is, the specifics. Supervisor A agrees with subordinate B, that B will work toward agreed objectives in the coming quarter and that evaluation of his or her work will take as a benchmark the objectives agreed to. Worthy objectives satisfactorily achieved will make for a productive relationship between A and B. This system does not appeal to diffuse cultures because they approach the issue from the opposite direction. It is the relationship between A and B that increases or reduces output, not the other way around. Objectives or specifics may be out of date by the time valuation comes around. B may not have performed as promised yet done something more valuable in altered circumstances. Only strong and lasting relationships can handle unexpected changes of this kind. Contracts and small print face backward in such cultures. In a specific culture companies use feedback and criticism talks as management tools which don't endanger personal relationships. In diffuse cultures, a public receiving and confess with criticism would mean a loss of face. As an example, a managing director of the Dutch 3M-subsidiary asked the participants of an employee's meeting for their feedback. It was harsh and quite aggressive. As the employees had to assess the event afterwards, she rated it from good to excellent. [67]

---

[66] Cf. Rothlauf (2012, pp. 55–56); Gutting (2016, pp. 57–58); Trompenaars and Hampden-Turner (2012, pp. 101–124)

[67] Cf. Trompenaars and Hampden-Turner (2012, pp. 101–121); Gutting (2016, pp. 59–61); Blom and Meier (2004, pp. 58–61)

Specific	Diffuse
Differences:	
- Rather 'open' public space, rather 'closed' private space. - Direct, to the point, purposeful in relating to others. - Precise, blunt, definitive and transparent. - Separates work and private life. - Principals and consistent oral stands independently of the person being addressed.	- Rather 'closed' public space, rather 'open private space. - Indirect, circuitous, seemingly 'aimless forms of relating to others. - Evasive, tactful, ambiguous, even opaque. - Work and private life are closely linked. - Highly situational morality depending upon the person and context encountered.
Tips for doing Business - Study the objectives, principles and numerical targets of the specific organization with which you are dealing - Be quick, to the point and efficient. - Structure the meeting with time intervals and agendas. - Do not use titles or acknowledge skills that are irrelevant to the issue being discussed. - Do not be offended by confrontations; they are usually not personal.	- Study the history, background, and future vision of the diffuse organization with which you expect to do business. - Take time, and remember there is more than one way to skin a cat. - Let the meeting flow, occasionally nudging its process. - Respect a person's title, age, and background connections, whatever issue is being discussed. - Do not get impatient when people are indirect or circuitous.
Managing and being Managed - Management is the realization of objectives and standards with rewards attached. - Private and business agendas are kept separate from each other. - Conflicts of interest are frowned on. - Clear, precise, and detailed instructions are seen as assuring better compliance, or as allowing employees to dissent in clear terms. - Begin reports with an executive summary.	- Management is a continuously improving process by which quality improves. - Private and business issues interpenetrate. - Consider an employee's whole situation before you judge him or her. - Ambiguous and vague instructions are seen as allowing subtle and responsive interpretations through which employees can exercise personal judgment. - End reports with a concluding overview.

Table 10: Specific vs. Diffuse[68]

---

[68] Adopted from Hoecklin (1998, p. 45); Trompenaars and Hampden-Turner (2012, pp. 123–124)

3.1.5 Achievement vs. Ascription

All societies give certain of their member's higher status than others, signaling that unusual attention should be focused on such people and their activities. This dimension relates to the question whether an individual's status is determined by gender, religion, origin or age; or whether it is mainly reached by own achievements. At a conference on a Japanese-Dutch joint venture held in Rotterdam, a Japanese participant fell ill. A member of the Dutch delegation approached another Japanese delegate and asked if he would replace the sick man. Mr. Yoshi demurred, and the Dutchman was annoyed at the lack of a straight response. Several minutes later the leader of the Japanese delegation announced that the delegate would replace the sick man, because he was appointing him to the task. It was made abundantly clear whose decision that had been. An achievement-oriented Swedish manager was managing a project in Pakistan. A vacancy needed to be filled and after careful assessment, the Swedish manager chose one of his two most promising Pakistani employees for promotion. Both candidates were highly educated, with Ph.D.'s in mechanical engineering, and in Pakistan, both were known authorities in their field. Although both had excellent performance records, Mr. Kahn was selected based on some recent achievements. Mr. Saran, the candidate not chosen, was upset by the turn of events. He went to his Swedish boss for an explanation. However, even an explanation based on the specific needs of the business did not calm him. The reason was the fact that Mr. Saran received his Ph.D. two years before Mr. Khan, from the same American university. Saran was expected to have more status than his colleague because of this. His family would never understand.[69]

Achievement	Ascription
Differences	
- Use of titles only when relevant to the competences you bring to the task. - Respect for superior in hierarchy is based on how effectively his or her job is done and how adequate their knowledge.	- Extensive use of titles, especially when these clarify your position in the organization. - Respect for superior in hierarchy is a measure of your commitment to the organization and its mission. - Most senior managers are male, middle-aged and qualified by their background.

---

[69] Cf. Trompenaars and Hampden-Turner (2012, pp. 125–145)

Achievement	Ascription
- Most senior managers are of varying age and gender and have shown proficiency in specific jobs.	
Tips for doing Business	
- Make sure your negotiation team has enough data, technical advisers, and knowledgeable people to convince the other company that the project, jointly pursued, will work.	- In order to convince the other company that you consider this negotiation important, make sure your negotiation team consist of enough older, senior officials, as well as others with formal titles.
- Respect the expertise and information of your counterparts even if you suspect they are short of influence back home.	- Respect the status and influence of your counterparts even if you suspect they lack experience. Do not make them feel foolish.
- Use the title that reflects how competent you are as an individual.	- Use the title that reflects your degree of influence in your organization.
- Do not underestimate the need of your counterparts to do better or do more than is expected. To challenge is to motivate.	- Do not underestimate the need of your counterparts to make their ascriptions come true. To challenge is to subvert.
Managing and being Managed	
- Respect for a manager is based on knowledge and skills.	- Respect for a manager is based on seniority.
- Management by objectives and pay-for-performance are effective tools	- Management by objectives and pay-for-performance are less effective than direct rewards from the manager.
- Decisions are challenged on technical and functional grounds.	- Decisions are challenged only by people with higher authority.

Table 11: Achievement vs. Ascription[70]

3.1.6 Human-Time-Relationship

Basically, this dimension is about the relative importance cultures give to the past, present, and future. Another similarity to Hall's model, thus it can be referred to the explanations in *part 1.1.3 and 1.2.3* of this assignment. In some cultures, time management is rather sequential, in others it's rather circular or synchronic. The sequentialistic approach, also called monochromic time, moves forward in a straight line. In the synchronistic approach, also called polychronic time, moves around in cycles of minutes, hours, days, weeks, months, and years. People structuring time sequentially tend to do one thing at a time. They view time as a

---

[70] Adopted from Hoecklin (1998, p. 121); Trompenaars and Hampden-Turner (2012, pp. 144–145)

narrow line of distinct, consecutive segments. They strongly prefer planning and keeping plans once they have been made, rather than extemporizing and adapting. Time commitments are taken seriously and staying on schedule is a must. Conversely, people structuring time synchronically usually do several things at a time. To them, time is a wide ribbon, allowing many things to take place simultaneously. Time is intangible and flexible. Time commitments are desirable rather than absolute. Plans are easily changed. Synchronic people especially value the satisfactory completion of interactions with others. Furthermore, the researcher distinguished between Past-, Present- and Future-oriented cultures.[71] To a synchronic person, not being greeted spontaneously and immediately, even while the other person is still talking on the telephone, is a slight. In a company that has quarterly intervals determining bonuses and merits, for synchronic cultures these intervals feel far to frequent while for sequential cultures they are perfect as rewards must closely follow the behavior they are intended to reinforce, otherwise you lose the connection. Synchronic cultures feel that this go-for-the-quick-buck philosophy has been loses customers as these don't like the pressure at the end of the quarter.[72] A Taiwanese worker traveled to the head-office of his employer in Germany. As he entered his bosses' office, the manager was currently on the phone. The boss gave his employer a sign, telling him to wait outside. The Taiwanese worker had absolutely no understanding for that. He felt deeply offended.[73]

Past Orientation	Present Orientation	Future Orientation
Differences		
- There is much talk about the history and origins of the family, business, and nation. - People are motivated to re-create a golden age. - Respect is shown for ancestors, predecessors, and older people.	- Activities and enjoyments of the moment are most important. - Plans are not objected to but are rarely executed. - Intense interest is shown in present	- There is much talk about prospects, potentials, aspirations, and future achievements. - Planning and strategizing are

---

[71] Cf. Trompenaars and Hampden-Turner (2012, pp. 147–172); Rothlauf (2012, p. 57); Trompenaars and Dumetz (2012, pp. 153–162)
[72] Cf. Trompenaars and Hampden-Turner (2012, p. 153)
[73] Cf. Rentzsch (1999, p. 61)

Past Orientation	Present Orientation	Future Orientation
- Everything is viewed in the context of tradition or history.	relationships, "here and now." - Everything is viewed in terms of its contemporary impact and style.	done enthusiastically. - Intense interest is shown in youthfulness and in future potentials. - The present and past are used, even exploited, for the future.
Tips for doing Business - Emphasize the history, tradition, and rich cultural heritage of those you deal with as evidence of their vast potential. - Discover whether internal relationships will sanction the kind of changes you seek to encourage. - Agree to future meetings in principle, but do not fix deadlines for completion. - Do your homework on the history, traditions, and past glories of the company; consider what reenactments you might propose.		- Emphasize the freedom, opportunity, and limitless scope for the company and its people in the future. - Discover what core competence or continuity the company intends to carry with it into the envisaged future. - Agree to specific deadlines, and do not expect work to be completed unless you have set such deadlines. - Do your homework on the future, the prospects, and the technological potentials of the company; consider mounting a sizable challenge.

Table 12: Past- / Present- / Future-Orientation[74]

---

[74] Adopted from Trompenaars and Hampden-Turner (2012, p. 170)

Sequential/Monochrome	Synchronic
Differences	
- Do only one activity at a time.	- Do more than one activity at a time.
- Time is sizable and measurable	- Appointments are approximate and subjects to 'giving time' to significant others
- Keep appointments strictly; schedule in advance and do not run late.	- Schedules are generally subordinate to relationships.
- Relationships are generally subordinate to the schedule.	- Strong preference for following where relationships lead.
- Strong preference for following initial plans.	
Managing and being Managed	
- Employees feel rewarded and fulfilled by achieving planned future goals as in management by objectives.	- Employees feel rewarded and fulfilled by achieving improved relationships with supervisors and customers.
- Employees' most recent performance is the major issue, along with whether their commitments for the future can be relied on.	- Employees' whole history with the company and future potential is the context in which their current performance is viewed.
- Plan the career of an employee jointly with him or her, stressing landmarks to be reached by certain times.	- Discuss with the employee his or her final aspirations in the context of the company; in what ways can these be realized?
- The corporate ideal is the straight line and the most direct, efficient and rapid route to your objectives.	- The corporate ideal is the interacting circle in which past experience, present opportunities, and future possibilities interact.
Examples	
- Philippines	- China
- Ireland	- Hong Kong
- Brazil	- South Korea

Table 13: Sequential vs. Synchronic[75]

3.1.7 Human-Nature Relationship

Trompenaars and Hampden-Turner also examined the ways in which people deal with their environment. Specific attention should be given to whether they believe in controlling outcomes (inner-directed) or letting things take their own course (outer-directed). Societies either believe that they can and should control nature by imposing their will on it or they believe that humans are part of nature and must go along with its laws, directions, and forces. The first of these orientations should be described as inner-directed (internal control). This kind of

---

[75] Adopted from Trompenaars and Hampden-Turner (2012, p. 143); Engelen and Tholen (2014, p. 68)

culture tends to identify with mechanisms; that is, the organization is conceived of as a machine that obeys the will of its operators. The second, the outer-directed (external control), tends to see an organization as itself a product of nature, owing its development to the nutrients in its environment and to favorable ecological balance. It is necessary to say, that outer directed doesn't mean god-directed or fate-directed; it may mean directed by the knowledge revolution or by the looming pollution crisis, or by a joint-venture partner. The ideal is to fit advantageously to an external force.[76] An example is the history of the *Sony Walkman*. In an interview, Sony's Akio Moriata explained that he conceived of the notion of the Walkman while he was searching for a way to enjoy music without disturbing others. This impetus is in sharp contrast to the normal motivation for using a *Walkman* in northwestern Europe and North America, where most users do not want to be disturbed by other people.[77] A pay-for-performance program assumes that each employee can behave in ways that that increase the sales of e.g. computers, that he or she can personally induce greater effort and hence greater sales. This assumes is questioned by employees who believe in external control. For them it leads to customers being overloaded with products they never wanted and do not need. Furthermore, when things are not going well for our people, it is a mistake to hurry or blame them. There are good times and bad times. Paying them for performance does not change inevitable trends.[78]

Internal control	External control
Differences	
- Often dominant attitude bordering on aggressiveness towards the environment. - Conflict and resistance means that you have convictions. - Focus is on oneself, one's own group and organization. - Discomfort when environment seems 'out of control' or changeable.	- Often flexible attitude, willing to compromise and keep the peace. - Harmony and responsiveness, that is, sensibility. - Focus is on 'others', that is customer, partner, colleague. - Comfort with waves, shifts, cycles if these are natural.
Tips for doing Business	

---

[76] Cf. Hodgetts, Luthans, and Doh (2006, p. 130); Trompenaars and Hampden-Turner (2012, pp. 173–191); Rothlauf (2012, pp. 57–58)
[77] Cf. Trompenaars and Hampden-Turner (2012, p. 178)
[78] Cf. Trompenaars and Hampden-Turner (2012, pp. 183–184)

Internal control	External control
- Playing "hardball" is legitimate to test the resilience of an opponent. - It is most important to "win your objective." - Win some, lose some.	- Softness, persistence, politeness, and long, long patience will get rewards. - It is most important to "maintain your relationship." - Win together, lose apart.
Managing and being Managed	
- Get agreement on and ownership of clear objectives. - Make sure that tangible goals are clearly linked to tangible rewards. - Discuss disagreements and conflicts openly; they show that everyone is determined. - Management by objectives works if all parties genuinely committed to directing themselves toward shared objectives and if these objectives persist.	- Achieve congruence among various people's goals. - Try to reinforce the current directions and facilitate the work of employees. - Give people time and opportunity to quietly work through conflicts, which are distressing. - Management by environments works if all parties are genuinely committed to adapting themselves to fit external demands as these demands shift.
Examples	
- USA - Australia	- Egypt - Thailand

Table 14: Internal vs. External control[79]

---

[79] Adopted from: Trompenaars and Hampden-Turner (2012, pp. 190–191); Engelen and Tholen (2014, p. 69)

4. References

Airports Council International. (2015). Year to date Passenger Trafic. Retrieved March 23, 2017, from http://www.aci.aero/Data-Centre/Monthly-Traffic-Data/Passenger-Summary/Year-to-date.

Altunisik, M., & Tür, Ö. (2004). *Turkey: Challenges of Continuity and Change (The Contemporary Middle East)* (1st ed.). Oxon: Routledge.

Ari, A., & Cergibozan, R. (2016). The twin crises: Determinants of banking and currency crises in the Turkish economy. *Emerging markets finance & trade : a journal of the Society for the Study of Emerging Markets, 52*(1/3), 123–135.

Berger, T., & Hagemann, K. (2011). *Intercultural Management and Communication: Study Letter* (1. Auflage). Riedlingen: SRH FernHochschule.

Berndt, W. (2015). *Kleines Handbuch Türkei: Gesellschaft, Geschichte, Politik, Wirtschaft* (1. Auflage). Rostock: Ramses Verlag.

Blom, H., & Meier, H. (2004). *Interkulturelles Management: Interkulturelle Kommunikation. Internationales Personalmanagement. Diversity-Ansätze im Unternehmen* (2. Auflage). Herne: NWB Verlag.

Bluenomics. (2017). Structure of gross value added by sectors (GVA) - Turkey. Retrieved March 23, 2017, from https://www.bluenomics.com/data#!data/national_accounts_gdp/gdp_production_approach/structure_of_gross_value_added_by_sectors_gva_/901686967!chart/line&countries=turkey.

Butler, D. (2012). UPDATE 4-Turkey regains investment grade rating after long wait. Retrieved March 23, 2017, from http://www.reuters.com/article/turkey-fitch-rating-idUSL5E8M56DZ20121105.

Carlson, S. (2013). Moody's upgrades Turkey's government bond ratings to Baa3, stable outlook. Retrieved March 23, 2017, from Moody's Investor Service: https://www.moodys.com/research/Moodys-upgrades-Turkeys-government-bond-ratings-to-Baa3-stable-outlook--PR_273186.

Carté, P., & Fox, C. (2004). *Bridging the culture gap: A practical guide to international business communication*. London: Kogan Page.

Central Intelligence Agency. (2017). The World Factbook: Middle East: Turkey. Retrieved March 11, 2017, from https://www.cia.gov/library/publications/the-world-factbook/geos/tu.html.

Dombey, D. (2013a). Iraq: Ankara views country as 'natural extension' for business. Retrieved March 23, 2017, from https://www.ft.com/content/64635cd4-ae7e-11e2-bdfd-00144feabdc0#axzz2Sv1nMx5G.

Dombey, D. (2013b). Silk roads lead to Turkey's resurgent power: The New Trade Routes: Turkey. Retrieved March 23, 2017, from https://www.ft.com/content/63c7a992-ae7e-11e2-bdfd-00144feabdc0.

Dumetz, J. (Ed.). (2012). *Cross-cultural management textbook: Lessons from the world leading experts in cross-cultural management* (1st ed.): CreateSpace Independent Publishing Platform.

eDiplomat. (2015a). United States - Cultural Etiquette. Retrieved March 12, 2017, from http://www.ediplomat.com/np/cultural_etiquette/ce_us.htm.

eDiplomat. (2015b). France - Cultural Etiquette. Retrieved March 28, 2017, from http://www.ediplomat.com/np/cultural_etiquette/ce_fr.htm.

Engelen, A., & Tholen, E. (2014). *Interkulturelles Management*. Stuttgart: Schäffer-Poeschel.

Ertuğrul, A., & Selçuk, F. (2001). A brief account of the Turkish economy, 1980 - 2000. *Russian & East European finance and trade, 37*(6), 6–30.

Finkel, A. (2012). *Turkey: What Everyone Needs to Know* (1st ed.): Oxford University Press.

Finkel, I., & Harvey, B. (2014). Turkey Cut to Junk as Moody's Concludes Its Post-Coup Review. Retrieved March 23, 2017, from https://www.bloomberg.com/news/articles/2016-09-23/turkey-cut-to-junk-as-moody-s-concludes-its-post-coup-review.

Forbes Magazine. (2016). The World's Biggest Public Companies. Retrieved March 23, 2017, from https://www.forbes.com/global2000/list/#country:Turkey.

Fresh Plaza. (2016). EU imported 21% more fruit and veg from Turkey. Retrieved March 23, 2017, from http://www.freshplaza.com/article/170869/EU-imported-21-procent-more-fruit-and-veg-from-Turkey/.

Geromel, R. (2013). Forbes Top 10 Billionaire Cities: Moscow Beats New York Again. Retrieved March 23, 2017, from https://www.forbes.com/sites/ricardogeromel/2013/03/14/forbes-top-10-billionaire-cities-moscow-beats-new-york-again/2/#1f00d0db5b64.

Gutting, D. (2016). *Interkulturelles Management, Diversity und internationale Kooperation* (1st ed.). Herne: NWB Verlag.

Hall, E. T. (1963). A system for the notation of proxemic behavior. *American anthropologist, 65*(5), 1003–1026.

Hall, E. T. (1969). *The Hidden Dimension* (1st ed.). New York: Doubleday.

Hall, E. T. (1973). *The Silent Language* (1st ed.). New York: Anchor Books.

Hall, E. T., & Reed Hall, M. (1990). *Understanding cultural differences: Germans, French and Americans* (1st ed.). Boston: Harvard Business School Press.

Hall, E. T., & Reed Hall, M. (2001). Key Concepts: Underlying Strucutres of Culture. In M. H. Albrecht (Ed.), *International HRM. Managing Diversity in the Workplace* (1st ed., pp. 24–40). Oxford: Blackwell Publishing.

Haller, P. M., & Nägele, U. (2013). *Praxishandbuch Interkulturelles Management: Der andere Weg: Affektives Vermitteln interkultureller Kompetenz* (2013rd ed., Vol. 1). Wiesbaden: Springer Gabler.

Hampden-Turner, C., & Trompenaars, A. (2000). *Building cross-cultural competence: How to create wealth from conflicting values*. Chichester: John Wiley.

Hershlag, Z. Y. (1968). *Turkey: The challenge of growth* (2nd ed.). Leiden: Brill.

Hodge, S. (2000). *Global Smarts: The art of communicating and deal making anywhere in the world* (1st ed.). New York: John Wiley & Sons, Inc.

Hodgetts, R. M., Luthans, F., & Doh, J. P. (2006). *International management: Culture, strategy, and behavior* (6th ed.). Boston: McGraw-Hill.

Hoecklin, L. A. (1998). *Managing cultural differences: Strategies for competitive advantage* (Reprint). *The EIU series*. Wokingham: Addison-Wesley.

Hollensen, S. (2007). *Global marketing: A decision-oriented approach* (4th ed.). Harlow: Financial Times Prentice Hall.

International Monetary Fund. (2017). GDP Turkey. Retrieved March 22, 2017, from
http://www.imf.org/external/pubs/ft/weo/2016/01/weodata/weorept.aspx?sy=1980&ey=2021&scsm=1&ssd=1&sort=country&ds=.&br=1&pr1.x=44&pr1.y=16&c=186&s=NGDPD%2CNGDPDPC%2CPPPGDP%2CPPPPC%2CPPPSH%2CLUR%2CLP&grp=0&a=.

Investment Support and Promotion Agency of Turkey. (2013). The Logistics Industry in Turkey. Retrieved March 23, 2017, from
http://www.invest.gov.tr/en-US/infocenter/publications/Documents/TRANSPORTATION-LOGISTICS-INDUSTRY.pdf.

Investment Support and Promotion Agency of Turkey. (2014). Turkey's Machine Industry. Retrieved March 23, 2017, from http://www.invest.gov.tr/en-US/infocenter/publications/Documents/MACHINERY.INDUSTRY.pdf.

Investment Support and Promotion Agency of Turkey. (2017a). Agriculture and Food. Retrieved March 24, 2017, from http://www.invest.gov.tr/en-US/sectors/Pages/Agriculture.aspx.

Investment Support and Promotion Agency of Turkey. (2017b). Foreign Trade. Retrieved March 24, 2017, from http://www.invest.gov.tr/en-US/investmentguide/investorsguide/Pages/InternationalTrade.aspx.

Investment Support and Promotion Agency of Turkey. (2017c). Tourism - Invest in Turkey. Retrieved March 23, 2017, from http://www.invest.gov.tr/en-US/sectors/Pages/WellnessAndTourism.aspx.

Investment Support and Promotion Agency of Turkey. (2017d). TR - Snapshot - Invest in Turkey. Retrieved March 23, 2017, from http://www.invest.gov.tr/en-US/turkey/factsandfigures/Pages/TRSnapshot.aspx.

Investment Support and Promotion Agency Turkey. (2014). Turkey's Automotive Industry. Retrieved March 23, 2017, from
http://www.invest.gov.tr/en-US/infocenter/publications/Documents/AUTOMOTIVE.INDUSTRY.pdf.

Kardas, S. (2009). Turkish recovery needs more time. Retrieved March 23, 2017, from http://www.atimes.com/atimes/Central_Asia/KH25Ag01.html.

Katırcıoğlu, S. T., & Feridun, M. (2011). Do macroeconomic fundamentals affect exchange market pressure?: Evidence from bounds testing approach for Turkey. *Applied economics letters, 18*(1/3), 295–300.

Kılınç, M., Kılınç, Z., & Turhan, M. I. (2012). Resilience of the Turkish economy during the global financial crisis of 2008. *Emerging Markets Finance and Trade, 48*(5), 19–34.

Koç Holding. (2017). About. Retrieved March 22, 2017, from Koç Holding: http://www.koc.com.tr/en-us/about.

Kumbruck, C., & Derboven, W. (2016). *Interkulturelles Training: Trainingsmanual zur Förderung interkultureller Kompetenzen in der Arbeit* (3rd ed.). Berlin: Springer.

Matveev, A. (2016). *Intercultural Competence in Organizations: A Guide for Leaders, Educators and Team Players* (1st ed.). Wiesbaden: Springer.

Mezzofiore, G. (2014). Erdogan Airport: Istanbul's Super Hub 'to be Named After Turkey's President-Elect'. Retrieved March 23, 2017, from http://www.ibtimes.co.uk/erdogan-airport-istanbuls-super-hub-be-named-after-turkeys-president-elect-1461166.

Moll, M. (2012). *The Quintessence of Intercultural Business Communication* (2012nd ed.). Heidelberg: Springer.

Müller, S., & Gelbrich, K. (2013). *Interkulturelle Kommunikation* (1st ed.). München: Vahlen.

Nordea Trade. (2017). The economic context of Turkey. Retrieved March 24, 2017, from https://www.nordeatrade.com/dk/explore-new-market/turkey/economical-context?

n-tv. (2017). Nur noch Ramschniveau: Fitch senkt Türkei-Rating. Retrieved March 24, 2017, from http://www.n-tv.de/wirtschaft/Fitch-senkt-Tuerkei-Rating-article19671312.html.

OECD. (2017a). OECD Data. Retrieved March 11, 2017, from The Organisation for Economic Co-operation and Development: https://data.oecd.org/.

OECD. (2017b). Labour force participation rate: OECD Data. Retrieved March 22, 2017, from https://data.oecd.org/emp/labour-force-participation-rate.htm.

PwC Turkey. (2011). Doing Business in Turkey. Retrieved March 23, 2017, from PwC Turkey: https://www.pwc.com.tr/tr/publications/arastirmalar/pdf/doing_business_in_tu rkey_-_dusuk.pdf.

Rentzsch, H.-P. (1999). *Erfolgreich verhandeln im weltweiten Business: Verhalten, Taktik und Strategie für internationale Meetings und Präsentationen* (1st ed.). Wiesbaden: Gabler Verlag.

Republic of Turkey Prime Ministry Investment Support and Promotion Agency. (2014). Electronics Sector in Turkey, from Republic of Turkey Prime Ministry Investment Support and Promotion Agency: http://www.invest.gov.tr/en-US/infocenter/publications/Documents/ELECTRONICS.INDUSTRY.pdf.

Republic of Turkey. Ministry of Economy. (2016). Clothing Industry. Retrieved http://www.ekonomi.gov.tr/portal/content/conn/UCM/path/Contribution%20Fol ders/web_en/Home/Sectoral%20Reports%20and%20Statistics/Sectoral%20 Reports/Industry/hg-clothing.pdf, from.

Rothlauf, J. (2012). *Interkulturelles Management: Mit Beispielen aus Vietnam, China, Japan, Russland und den Golfstaaten* (4th ed.). München: Oldenbourg Verlag.

Rothlauf, J. (2014). *A Global View on Intercultural Management: Challenges in a Globalized World* (1st ed.): Oldenbourg.

Sabancı Holding. (2017). Sabancı Group. Retrieved March 21, 2017, from Sabancı Holding: https://sabanci.com/en/sabanci-group/k-50.

Sano, A. (2017). Turkish auto exports hit 1m for first time in 2016- Nikkei Asian Review. Retrieved March 23, 2017, from http://asia.nikkei.com/Politics-Economy/Economy/Turkish-auto-exports-hit-1m-for-first-time-in-2016/.

Sansal, B. (2016). Kemalism - All About Turkey. Retrieved March 29, 2017, from http://www.allaboutturkey.com/ata_prensip.htm.

Schuß, H. (2012). Wirtschaftliche Entwicklung von der Gründung der Republik bis heute. In U. Steinbach (Ed.), *Länderbericht Türkei* (1282nd ed., pp. 328–368). Bundeszentrale für politische Bildung.

Sharkov, D. (2014). Istanbul's New Erdoğan-Backed Airport to Be Named
    After... Erdoğan. Retrieved March 23, 2017, from
    http://europe.newsweek.com/istanbuls-new-erdogan-backed-airport-be-
    named-after-erdogan-264580?rm=eu.

Sonmez, M. (2017). Why 2017 doesn't bode well for Turkey's economy.
    Retrieved March 23, 2017, from Al Monitor: http://www.al-
    monitor.com/pulse/originals/2017/01/turkey-economy-black-winter-
    alarm.html.

SRH FernHochschule. (2014). *Country Profile USA: Studienbrief* (1st ed.).
    Riedlingen.

The Economist. (2009). Turkey's fragile economy: Fund management.
    Retrieved March 22, 2017, from http://www.economist.com/node/14041662.

The Economist. (2010). Stockmarkets. Retrieved March 23, 2017, from
    http://www.economist.com/node/15213745.

The Heritage Foundation. (2017). Index of Economic Freedom. Retrieved
    March 24, 2017, from http://www.heritage.org/index/heatmap.

The World Bank. (2017). Turkey: Country at a Glance. Retrieved March 22,
    2017, from http://www.worldbank.org/en/country/turkey.

Ting-Toomey, S., & Kurogi, A. (1998). Facework competence in intercultural
    conflict: An updated face-negotiation theory. *International journal of
    intercultural relations, 22*(2), 187–225.

Trompenaars, A., & Coebergh, P. H. (2015). *100+ management models: How
    to understand and apply the world's most powerful business tools* (1st ed.).
    New York: McGraw-Hill.

Trompenaars, A., & Hampden-Turner, C. (2012). *Riding the waves of culture:
    Understanding diversity in global business* (3rd ed.). London: Nicholas
    Brealey.

Trompenaars, F., & Dumetz, J. (2012). Cultural Dimensins Relating to Time. In
    J. Dumetz (Ed.), *Cross-cultural management textbook. Lessons from the
    world leading experts in cross-cultural management* (1st ed., pp. 147–167).
    CreateSpace Independent Publishing Platform.

Unver, H. A. (2016). The Real Challenge to Turkey's Economy Isn't Terrorism. Retrieved March 24, 2017, from https://hbr.org/2016/07/the-real-challenge-to-turkeys-economy-isnt-terrorism.

Veldhuizen, R. (2017). 2017 Preview: The lira and Turkey's risky debt. Retrieved March 24, 2017, from http://globalriskinsights.com/2017/01/2017-preview-turkeys-mounting-risks/.

Workman, D. (2017). Turkey's Top 10 Imports. Retrieved March 24, 2017, from http://www.worldstopexports.com/turkeys-top-10-imports/.

World Bank. (2017). Data - GDP Turkey - 1960-2015. Retrieved March 21, 2017, from http://data.worldbank.org/indicator/NY.GDP.MKTP.CD?end=2015&locations=TR&start=1960&view=chart.

WorldBusinessCulture.com. Background To Business in France. Retrieved March 28, 2017, from http://www.worldbusinessculture.com/French-Business-Style.html.

WorldBusinessCulture.com. (2017a). American Dress Code. Retrieved March 31, 2017, from http://www.worldbusinessculture.com/American-Business-Dress-Style.html.

WorldBusinessCulture.com. (2017b). Business Communication Styles in France. Retrieved April 01, 2017, from http://www.worldbusinessculture.com/French-Business-Communication-Style.html.

WorldBusinessCulture.com. (2017c). French Business Structures. Retrieved March 28, 2017, from http://www.worldbusinessculture.com/French-Business-Structures.html.

Xie, Y., Gokoluk, & Selcuk. (2013). Turkey Raised to Investment Grade by Moody's on Debt Cuts. Retrieved March 23, 2017, from https://www.bloomberg.com/news/articles/2013-05-16/turkey-raised-to-investment-grade-by-moody-s-on-debt-cuts.

Xiuqiong, W., & Jinfa, Z. (2009). Turkey's economy sees recovery signs as risks remain. Retrieved March 22, 2017, from http://news.xinhuanet.com/english/2009-06/28/content_11612750.htm.

Yong, L., & Baocheng, L. (2005). Cultural Differences and Clashes
in Communication. In J. Reuvid & L. Yong (Eds.), *Doing Business with China*
(5th ed., pp. 158–166). London: GMB Pulishing.

Zeldin, T. (1997). *The French* (2nd ed.). London: The Harvill Press.